In memory of my mother, Susan, an artist who sowed a beautiful garden —L.R.

To those who write, draw, sew, or sow —H.H.

"Georgia O'Keeffe in the Garden" Photo by Maria Chabot. © 2022 Georgia O'Keeffe Museum / Artists Rights Society (ARS), New York

Georgia O'Keeffe, Recipe card. © 2022 Georgia O'Keeffe Museum / Artists Rights Society (ARS), New York

Neal Porter Books

Text copyright © 2024 by Lisa Robinson

Illustrations copyright © 2024 by Hadley Hooper

All Rights Reserved

HOLIDAY HOUSE is registered in the U.S. Patent and Trademark Office.

Printed and bound in November 2023 at Toppan Leefung, DongGuan City, China.

The artwork for this book was created with traditional pen, paint, and paper and then assembled in Photoshop.

Book design by Jennifer Browne

www.holidayhouse.com

First Edition

1   3   5   7   9   10   8   6   4   2

Library of Congress Cataloging-in-Publication Data is available.

ISBN: 978-0-8234-5266-8   (hardcover)

Gifts from Georgia's Garden

How Georgia O'Keeffe Nourished Her Art

Lisa Robinson   Hadley Hooper

NEAL PORTER BOOKS

HOLIDAY HOUSE / NEW YORK

Georgia painted flowers so lush and
large they filled the canvas—
petunias, poppies, lilies,
and more . . .

"When you take a
flower in your hand
and really look at it,"
she said, "it's your
world for
the moment.

I want to give
that world to
someone else."

When Georgia looked, she saw a drop of dew on a stem, the pale vein of a leaf, the sensuous curl of a petal . . .

"Most people in the city rush around so, they have no time to look at a flower . . ."

"I will make even busy New Yorkers take time to see what I see of flowers."

But Georgia grew
tired of the city—
the cars,
crowds,
and skyscrapers.

She fled,

to a place she could feel free.
New Mexico.

Canyons,
mesas,
and skyscapes
welcomed her to her new home.

There, Georgia knelt and plunged
her hands down deep into the ground.
The scent of the soil unearthed memories
of growing up on a farm in Wisconsin—
colors and shapes and spaces.

The golden shimmer of a field of wheat;
rectangular rocks, twisted sticks, oval leaves;
barns with haylofts, windows, and doors.

Memories of a girl who announced in eighth grade,
"I'm going to be an artist."

And so,
beneath the wide skies of New Mexico,
inside adobe walls,
within this artist's imagination,
the seed of an idea took root:
to grow a garden.

A garden of her own.

First came a ring of fruit trees—
apple, peach, pear, apricot, cherry.

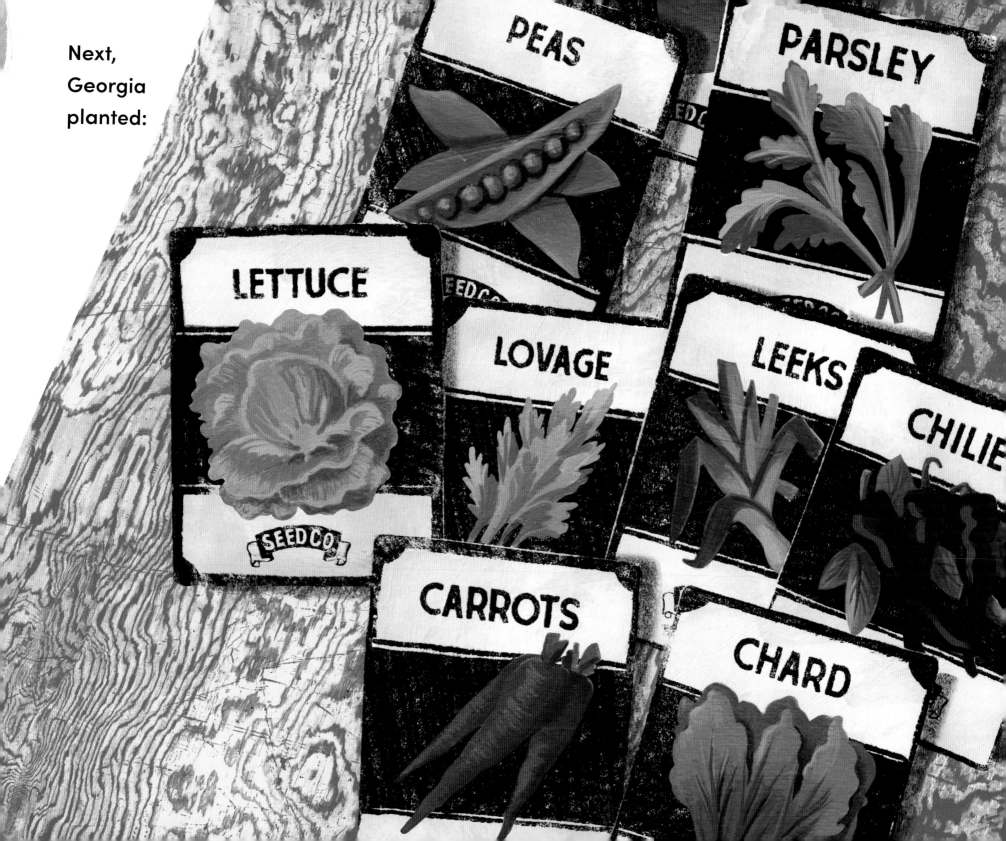

Next,
Georgia
planted:

PEAS

PARSLEY

LETTUCE

SEEDCO

LOVAGE

LEEKS

CHILIE

CARROTS

CHARD

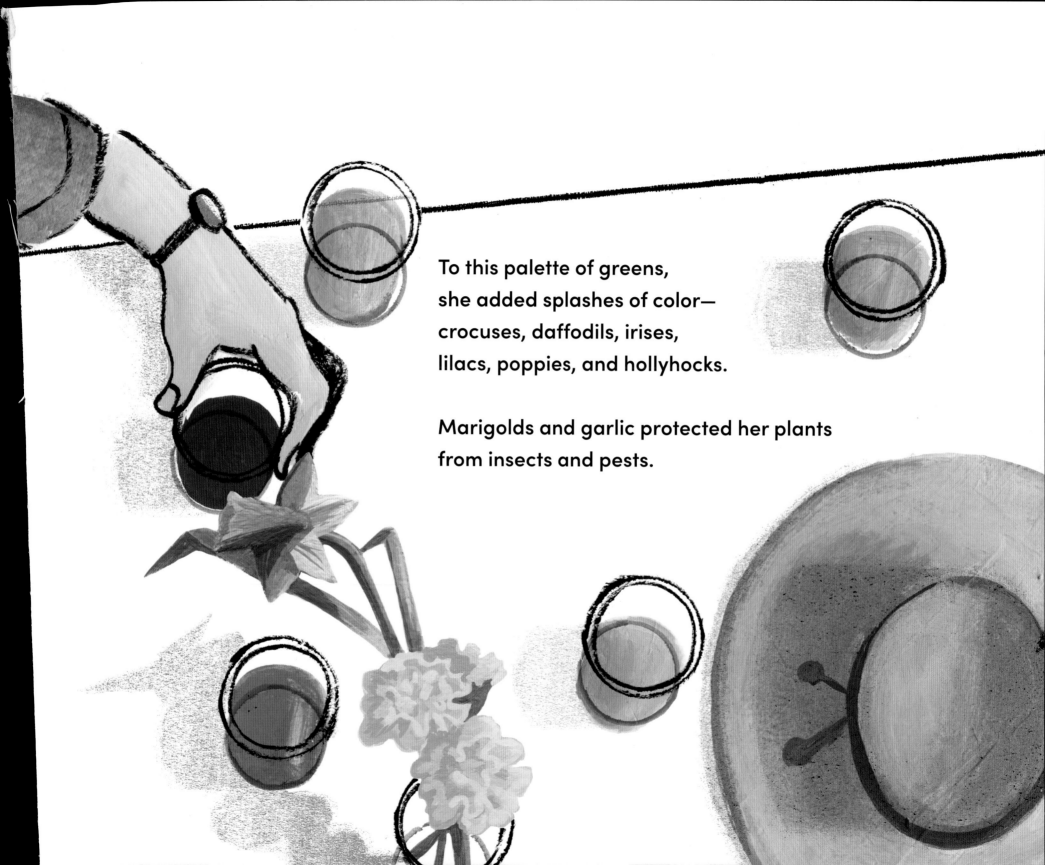

To this palette of greens,
she added splashes of color—
crocuses, daffodils, irises,
lilacs, poppies, and hollyhocks.

Marigolds and garlic protected her plants
from insects and pests.

While she waited for the seeds to sprout, Georgia painted.

And as the seedlings grew . . .
Georgia explored the nearby hills,
cliffs, and villages,
and painted.

And grew . . .
Georgia stitched cotton and linen
and wool, and painted.

And grew . . .
Georgia gathered rocks, collected skulls and bones,
and painted.

Finally, when her garden bloomed,
she fed herself and her friends with its gifts . . .
simple soups—
minestrone, potato and leek;

salads—
watercress or beet and bean;
dinner dishes—
tomato soufflé and green chile enchiladas.

After a meal, she might serve a delicious dessert,
like biscochitos—shortbread cookies with cinnamon sugar—
apple pie with pecans and whipped cream, or pecan butterballs.

1 cup butter   cream & knead)
1/4 " honey
2 " sifted flour
1/2 teaspoon salt
2 " " vanilla   Pecan Balls
2 cup finely chopped pecans
form in very small balls bake at 300
40-45 min roll hot in powdered sugar roll cold

Georgia bought local eggs and honey and goat milk.

She ground grain for homemade bread.

She hired members of the community to help with her household.

And all the while,
she painted.

The art of caretaking—
of her home and her garden—
nourished Georgia's art-making.

Georgia grew old in her garden
sanctuary, and even when she
became blind, she continued
to tend her garden
and paint.

To Georgia, everything was art,
and art was everything.
This vision was her gift to the world.
And her garden still grows today.

Georgia gardening in New Mexico, circa 1944

Who was Georgia O'Keeffe?

Georgia O'Keeffe was an American artist whose art, particularly her paintings of flowers, bones, and desert landscapes, received worldwide recognition. Georgia's creativity infused all aspects of her life, from cooking and gardening to sewing her clothing and decorating her home. Georgia was born in 1887 and raised on a farm in Wisconsin where she developed her love of wide skies and sweeping vistas. She knew from an early age that she wanted to become an artist, but it was difficult for women to enter the male-dominated art world of the early 1900s. Georgia persisted, however, and her dedication to developing her own expressive style ultimately earned her widespread respect and admiration. In her early forties, Georgia visited New Mexico, where she found inspiration in the dramatic desert setting. In 1945 she purchased her home in Abiquiú and it was here that she planted the garden that still thrives today.

What is sustainable gardening?

Georgia's reverence for nature spurred her to use sustainable gardening strategies. Sustainable gardening means gardening in a way that protects, rather than harms, the earth. Here are a few examples of how to grow a garden and take care of the earth at the same time.

Water conservation

Water is a precious resource. Water plants only when they need it. Use rainwater collected in barrels. Water plants in the early morning or evening when it's cooler so there is less water loss to evaporation.

Companion planting

Instead of using poisonous chemicals to ward off pests and disease, choose plants that help one another survive. For example, Georgia planted marigolds and garlic to repel harmful insects. Tall corn plants can provide shade for lettuce. Beans and peas enrich the soil.

Attract beneficial insects

Many insects help gardens grow. Bees are powerful pollinators and their presence increases the yield of plants like peppers, cucumbers, strawberries, and blueberries. Ladybugs, drawn to dandelions, will eat unwanted aphids. Dill attracts lacewings that eat aphids and mealybugs.

Composting

Composting food waste keeps it out of landfills and provides fertilizer for your garden. Save kitchen scraps, weeds, and leaf cuttings and put them in a composting bin. Once it's ready, add it to your garden.

Can I try one of Georgia's recipes?

A story in the *New York Times* about the sale of Georgia's handwritten recipe cards inspired me to write this story. Georgia enjoyed cooking with the fruits, vegetables, and herbs she grew in her garden.

Here's one of Georgia's cookie recipes you can try at home, adapted from the one you can see written in her own handwriting in this book:

Pecan Butterballs

1 cup butter

¼ cup sifted flour

½ teaspoon salt

2 teaspoons vanilla

2 cups finely chopped pecans

Powdered sugar for rolling cookies

Preheat the oven to 300 °F. Cream the butter and add the rest of the ingredients. Form the dough into small balls, place them on a baking sheet, and bake for 40–45 minutes. Roll the hot cookies in powdered sugar, then cool and roll in the powdered sugar again. Enjoy!

Sources

Cowart, Jack, and Juan Hamilton. *Georgia O'Keeffe: Art and Letters*. New York: New York Graphic Society, 1990.

Garcia, Maria. "Georgia O'Keeffe Exhibition Reveals A Fashion Icon Who Never Conformed To Anyone's Gaze." *WBUR*, December 15, 2017. https://www.wbur.org/artery/2017/12/15/georgia-okeeffe-style.

Georgia O'Keeffe: Exhibition of Oils and Pastels. An American Place, 509 Madison Ave, New York City, January 22–March 17, 1939. https://collections.library.yale.edu/catalog/15818083.

Lisle, Laurie. *Portrait of an Artist: A Biography of Georgia O'Keeffe*. New Mexico: University of New Mexico Press, 1986.

Lynes, Barbara Buhler & Agapita Judy Lopez. *Georgia O'Keeffe and Her Houses: Ghost Ranch and Abiquiu*. New York: Abrams, 2012.

Nierenberg, Amelia. "Own the Recipes of Georgia O'Keeffe." *New York Times*, February 7, 2020. https://www.nytimes.com/2020/02/07/dining/georgia-okeeffe-recipes.html.

O'Keeffe, Georgia. *Georgia O'Keeffe, A Studio Book*. New York: Viking Press, 1976.

Robinson, Roxana. *Georgia O'Keeffe: A Life*. New York: HarperCollins, 1989.

Wood, Margaret. *A Painter's Kitchen: Recipes from the Kitchen of Georgia O'Keeffe*. New Mexico: Museum of New Mexico Press, 2009.